About the Author

Mark W. Chamberlain, LLC

PhD: Pigheaded Determination®

Mark W. Chamberlain learned at an early age about **Vision Casting**, seeing the future and then creating it. He learned about the **Amish** and building communities around an idea, a project, a goal.

In 2011 he retired as vice president & financial advisor from Merrill Lynch. He took some trips, played some golf, walked on fire with Tony Robbins, and decided to create a university. His role model was Reverend Russell Conwell.

Reverend Russell Conwell talked about the fact that everyone, everywhere, all the time is surrounded by opportunity. We just need to work the fields. That talk, speech, and message became "**Acres of Diamonds.**" The proceeds from those speeches provided the seed money for Temple University.

Mark created **What If U Global™** to **Inspire**, **Instruct, Implement**. Inspire individuals to engage in **What If Thinking**. Instruct them, give them a strategy to create a plan. Implement the plan they constructed with **What If** Thinking.

His goal is to pass on what was given to him, to help people see the unseen, and then create it in partnership with individuals with a shared vision.

Inspire

Instruct

Implement

Copyright © 2016 Mark W. Chamberlain

All Rights Reserved

Dedication

Dedicated to the Women in My Life

Josephine Croop, Maternal Grandmother

Donna Chamberlain, Mother

Kathy M. Chamberlain, Wife of 41 Years

Kelly & Molly Chamberlain, Our Daughters

Terry Martin, Friend

Acknowledgements

Before any Dream can come true…

there must first be a Dream.

My maternal grandfather, Mark Croop, helped me see things that didn't exist. Today, some call that **Vision Casting**. He taught me about relationships and that the other person needs to win first. He taught me about the importance of asking—think Jabez*! *1 Chronicles 4:9–4:11*

It can be as simple as 1, 2, 3

1. **Vision Casting**, **What If** Thinking, Daydreaming
2. Relationships, Amish Barn Raising, **Win-Win**
3. Jabez, Ask to Expand Our Borders So We Can Increase Our Service

I Want You to Win **Big!**

YOU WIN … I WIN

---

*Jabez cried out to the God of Israel, "Oh, that you would bless me and enlarge my territory! Let your hand be with me, and keep me from harm so I will be free from pain." And God granted his request.

Contents

1. In the Beginning — 1
2. Amish Is a Verb — 2
3. **Vision Casting** — 3
4. Reticular Activating System: Ruts, Routines & Results — 6
5. **What If** vs. i'm too — 7
6. ABCs — 8
7. Mark's Math — 9
8. Cosmic Board of Directors — 10
9. Secret Silos — 11
10. Food, Sex, Money — 14
11. Donor Duplication/Client Copier — 16
12. The Wheels on the Bus, Ideal Prospects by the Bus Load — 18
13. Acres of Diamonds & Glass Ceiling? — 21
14. FOCUS: Any Emotion, Any Time Bonus — 23
15. One in 1,000/One in 1,000,000 — 24
16. Special Thanks — 25

Mark Croop

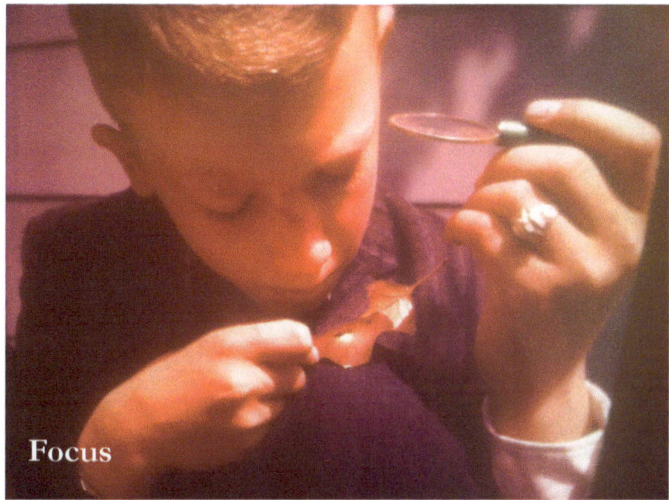

Focus

Teaching

1| In the Beginning

When I was young, my maternal grandfather, **Mark Croop**, gave me a magnifying glass and taught me how to use it. He said that simple glass was capable of creating intense heat and fire by simply focusing the rays of the sun on one thing.

We enlarge and magnify what we think about and focus on.

Think... What If | Passion, Joy, Love, Gratitude
vs.
i'm too, emotionless, sorrowful, hateful, ungrateful

He told me that it could help me **see things not seen by the naked eye**. Today we call that **Vision Casting**. He also taught me **the importance of sharing and teaching**.

2 | Amish Is a Verb

Mark Croop was a farmer, a politician. He taught me about the importance of "community" and the ability to create communities of like-minded individuals.

Think Amish

The Amish come together as a community to build barns for each other. They work toward a common goal, a common purpose.

What If

Think about your goals and creating communities of like-minded individuals. Give them an opportunity to use their skills, money, people, equipment, ideas, etc. to build **"barns"—YOUR "barns."**

Think Win-Win.

"Logic will get you from A to B. Imagination will take you anywhere."
Albert Einstein

3 | Vision Casting

What do you see?
When most people look at this picture, they see a swamp and some cows.

What If
1. My grandfather had lots of grandchildren. Summers are hot. My grandfather had lots of friends. Some of his friends had heavy equipment.

What is a swamp?

1. A swamp is a field with springs in it. This swamp had seven springs. My grandfather counted them as he walked around the field.

Think What If. Think Amish. Think Jabez.

My grandfather did some **What If Thinking** coupled with **Jabez**-like thinking and asked a friend to dredge out the swamp. That's me waving and my brother Jim on the other side.

The cost?
Just the effort involved in asking a friend for a hand.

Think Amish.

Amish is a Verb.

That's me and my grandfather. The dock isn't complete yet but he's getting dinner ready for the grandchildren. We did a lot of swimming that summer and many more.

I continue to build on those simple instructions.

1. Focus on one thing. That focus creates fire, passion. **Focus** can also create **any emotion, any time.** (More on this in the bonus chapter.)

2. Think about the **Amish** and the **building and creating of communities with shared vision, shared goals.**

3. I dedicate a couple hours a week to looking at things not seen by the naked eye. Vision Casting is seeing things that don't exist, unseen by the naked eye, and then creating them.

4 | Reticular Activating System | *Ruts, Routines & Results*

We are bombarded by stimuli all day: sight, smell, sound, touch. If we had to evaluate each stimulant, we would be frozen, consumed by the process. The human brain comes to the rescue.

The **Reticular Activating System** receives the stimuli and determines what's important and what isn't. We establish routines to make daily activity possible. We have favorites, preferences.

That's good, right?

The picture above is a picture of the **Wagon Wheel ruts** created when the wagon trains went west—the same way each time! **Google wagon wheel rut park** and you'll see evidence of this again and again.

Before you laugh too hard, we do the same thing with the help of our **Reticular Activating System**. At birth we speak no language, have no customs, no preferences. We establish these preferences, routines, and ruts over time. When the brain is presented with information and ideas that don't fit in these ruts, we generally discard them and continue—in the same routine, the same rut.

5 | What If **vs.** i'm too

Four statements **vs.** Four questions

i'm too
it's too
you're too
well, ya see

Remember the **reticular activating system?**

Too often we respond reflexively to new challenges, new ideas, with **learned behaviors.** The earth is round—fly like a bird, breathe under water, run a four-minute mile, put a man on the moon, perform a heart transplant, interpret speech recognition, invent self-driving cars; these were all concepts that seemed crazy, impossible. These behaviors and responses come reflexively. We don't think; we react, and we stay in the ruts.

What If?
How?
What If?
So What?

I suggest that if you substitute the second set of responses for the first, the results will amaze you.

There are some things to consider. People who don't, can't, or won't consider alternatives will tell you that you are crazy, dumb, and bound to fail. They will say it to your face and behind your back. And these are your friends and family. They don't want you to get hurt, be embarrassed, or lose.

Jack Canfield, the beloved originator of the Chicken Soup for the Soul® series, has personally taught millions of people his unique and modernized formulas for success and personal fulfillment and is a widely recognized leader in peak performance strategies.

He too knows doubt. "**What if** they read the book and think it's stupid, if it's not good or won't measure up?"[1]

---

[1] Bestseller Blueprint, Jack Canfield and Steve Harrison page 3 Module 1

6 | ABCs

A = Ask. If you are religious, take a look at the **Prayer of Jabez**. Very clearly we are told to make the ask—and regularly. If you are agnostic or atheist, ask. Think Babe Ruth. Step up and go for it.
A = Attitude. We are what we think about. If U think you can, U are right. If U think you can't, you are right.
A = Action. Get off the sidelines and in the game. U have to play to win.

B = Belief. If you believe there is no hope, you are right. If you believe there is hope, U R right.[2]
B = Behavior. If U act like a winner, U are. If you act like a loser, U R.
B = Benefits. If U act as if and believe U will succeed, chances are U will succeed

C= Choices. Remember **What If** vs. i'm too. Get in the game! Swing the bat. Take some hits. Go for it.
C = Consider. Darren Hardy, publisher of *Success* magazine, says, "I wish you Massive Failures." He understands if you go big, you will lose big—periodically. You can also win Big if you are in the game. Consider what you want and what you are willing to invest.
C = Consequences. Our attitudes and behaviors have consequences. If we believe there is no solution to our problems, guess what! If we behave like all is lost, guess what!

You can manage risk even if you go for the fences; you can manage, reduce, and possibly eliminate risk.

Think Amish. Think OPM.
[Other People's Money]

---

[5] You can reduce and in many cases eliminate the downside by employing "**The Amish Strategy**". Use Other People's Money, OPM.

7 | Mark's Math

$150 / 3 = **a.** $50   **b.** Whatever you want   **c.** Don't know

There is actually an infinite number of answers. All answers can be correct.

When I was in college, I got an apartment. The lease was in my name. It was a great apartment, great location, three bedrooms, living room, kitchen, nice bath. This was in the early '70s. The rent was $150 per month. I repeat: it was my apartment, my name on the lease.

What If?

I could simply divide $150 by 3 and come up with $50 for each person. Instead, I employed **What If Thinking** and charged each roommate $65. My cost per month was $20.

I refined that thinking and coupled that math with "**Amish Thought.**" I now create communities with shared values. My contribution is the idea and the creation of the community. The focus is the other person has to win first.

Whenever you have a cost, investment, or overhead, <u>think about individuals, businesses, and organizations that might benefit by participating in your venture</u>. The participation might be a monetary one, an in-kind investment, or an investment of machinery, people, or advertising. The possibilities are limited only by your imagination.

There are also a number of "funding" websites for individuals, nonprofits, and businesses. Google crowdfunding.

What If...

"The Ideals I stand for are not mine. I borrowed them from Socrates. I swiped them from Chesterfield. I stole them from Jesus. And I put them in a book. If you don't like their rules, whose would you use?"

Dale Carnegie

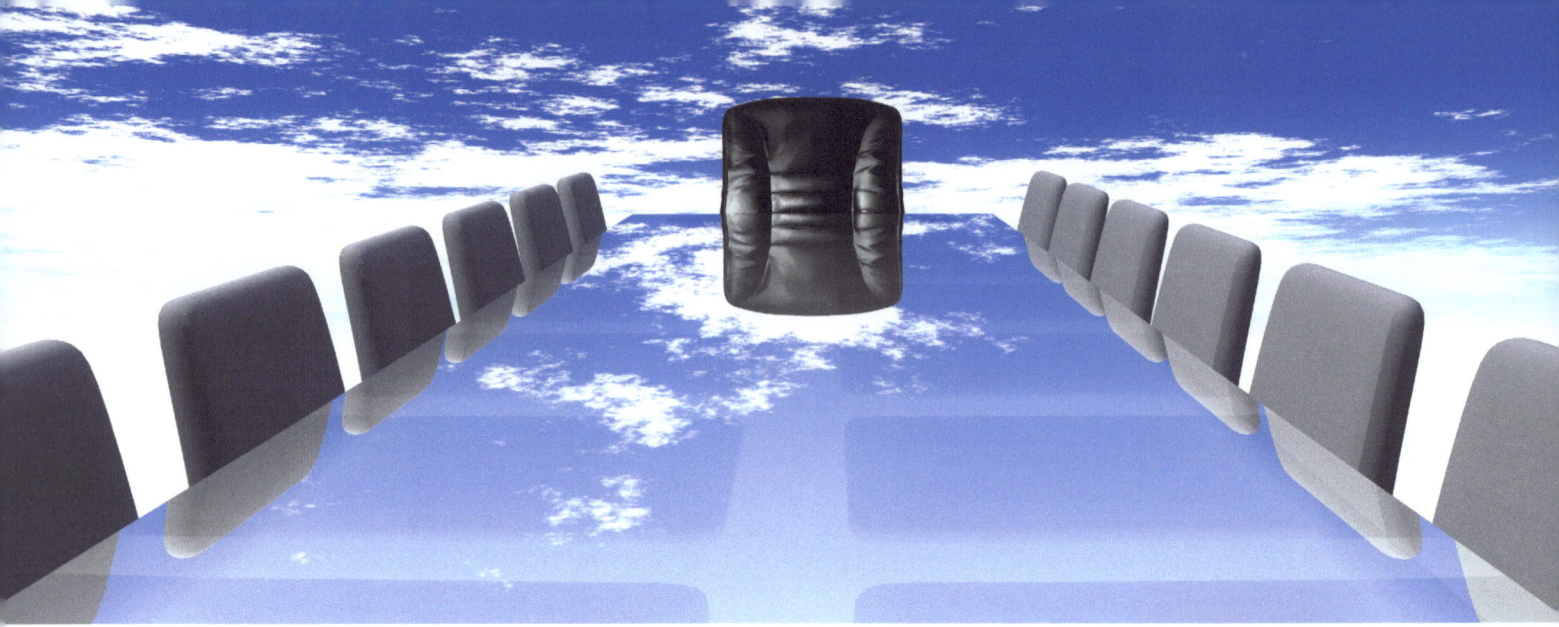

"They speak to me." John McCole Manager MONY

Me Explaining
The Cosmic Board of Director

8 | Cosmic Board of Directors

My first full-time job after college was with Mutual of New York. I was recruited by the regional manager, **John McCole**. He was an incredible person. There were a number of factors that contributed to his success. The first was his **client-centric** approach to the business. **Win-Win** was a phrase he used all the time. **"Our client has to win first. The client wins, then we win."**

He also had his office filled with pictures of historically famous individuals; most were deceased. When I asked John about their significance, he paused, smiled, and then said, **"They speak to me."** Dead people talking to my new employer? Had I made a mistake accepting his employment offer? He explained that he would look at the individuals and think about how they achieved the successes they had achieved. He used those lessons to take his business to ever higher levels of success.

I took his suggestion and that of Dale Carnegie. He too had a Cosmic Board of Directors: Socrates, Jesus, Chesterfield, etc.

Think about historically significant individuals. Think of inspirational individuals who achieved greatness. Put them on your Cosmic Board and listen to them.

Nelson Mandela, Mother Theresa, Lincoln, Margaret Thatcher, Eleanor Roosevelt, Martin Luther King, Jesus, Babe Ruth, Babe Dickerson, Steve Jobs, Winston Churchill, Ulysses S. Grant, and Sam Walton are some suggestions.

It's **Your Cosmic Board**; you decide. They are waiting to be called.

9 | Secret Silos
Time™, *NewsWeek*™, *Sports Illustrated*™, *US News & World Report*™

"Break your concept into its component parts. Research each individually. Watch out for the 'Dream Stealers'!"

Ken Pollock
Nice Guy, Businessman, Philanthropist, Vision Board Mastermind

Early in my career at Mutual of New York, I was told I needed to get my name out there. Sales is a contact sport. People advertise.

What If…

I knew I wanted to deal with professionals. I knew the geographic area I wanted to focus on. I knew the income level of those individuals. I researched the media and determined it could be productive to take out full-page ads in the above referenced media.

That is insane. New guy in the business who didn't have any money, any experience, taking out full-page ads in those national magazines?

I took John's advice and contacted Ken Pollock, a very successful local business person[3]. I practiced **What If Thinking**. **What If** he takes my call? **What If** he agrees to listen to me, then give counsel?

I made the call. He took the call. He listened.

Then he said this...
Always break your idea into its component parts[4]—advertising, production, raw materials, labor, marketing, etc. Research each component individually. Talk with experts in each area.
NEVER TELL ANYONE THE WHOLE STORY BECAUSE THEY WILL STEAL YOUR IDEA.

I smiled when he said *steal*. He paused and said, "**You don't understand. They will steal your thunder. They will say you are too young, too old, a minority, a woman, physically challenged, etc. Research the components. When and if you believe in the plan, go for it with the understanding that failures are guaranteed. It's part of the game. Learn from your mistakes, your failures, and go for it. I hope you have massive failures.**"

I was confused; massive failure? He explained life is like a pendulum, a metronome. **People who risk little, lose little and have small victories. If you want to win big, you will periodically lose big**[5].

He also talked about laughter. He said expect people to laugh at you and your **Awesome Dreams**. If you can handle the fact that periodically you will fail and people will laugh...

GO FOR IT!

---

[3] Ken Pollock is now on my **Cosmic Board of Directors**. He passed away but still guides me through his suggestions and encouragement.

[4] Mr. Pollock talked about breaking a business into its component parts. Being a farm boy, I heard silos. He suggested not telling anyone the whole picture; I heard secret. Secret Silos sounds more interesting than components.

In my research, I learned some national publications have regional editions so local advertisers can purchase only those markets they serve. You get the exposure and prestige of a national publication without the expense. Even a little guy like me could make the buy.

If I had listened to the laughter and not done my **What If research**, I would not have learned about market segmentation and market buys.

Break your idea into its component parts—Silos—and research each individually, especially the crazy ones. If you believe in the concept and can handle the laughter and failures, go for it.

Think Amish. **What If** you could spread your risk, allow others to invest in your success, and reduce or eliminate the downside? Over time I learned to expand my line of sight. I expanded my circle of friends, business partners, and potential business partners with a focus on their success. The other person or organization needs to have a win. It can be an emotional win. They may help or invest because they like you.

Think Jabez.

ASK

This is one of the magazines and full page ads I ran.

10. Food, Sex, Money
Mohegan Indians & Harvard Brain Research

We've covered a lot of ground. We've talked about **Vision Casting**, **Component Theory**, **Silos, and What If Thinking**. Here is an example of how they can come together.

The **Mohegan Indians** have a custom where they attach feathers to a stick. They call it a **talking stick**. The person holding the stick can't speak until he or she can repeat what has just been said; <u>first understand, then be understood</u>.

That is a powerful communications tool. The more you know about your prospects, clients, friends, the more you can help them Win.

You may say, "So what? Big deal." Stay with me.

Harvard University has conducted numerous studies on brain function. One of those studies suggests you can control brain function by reciting a series of three-word phrases. (You infer that after reading the studies.) Those phrases encourage speech. That speech stimulates that part of the brain that deals with Food, Sex, and Money.

Think about what I just said. You can "turn someone on" by using a series of three-word phrases.

You Control Their Brain Function

Harry Truman employed that tactic as he traveled around the US.

Hillary Clinton uses it now. Ever heard of the "**Listening Tours**"?

My grandfather, **Mark Croop**, taught me that at an early age. He was a Republican in a democratic district and won elections because he employed the techniques described in the Harvard studies. He knew it intuitively: <u>first understand, then be understood.</u>

11 | Donor Duplication | Client Copier

Think Amish
Think Jabez

"Get other people to fill a room at a private club with wealthy prospects, get other people to work the event for free, and get someone to cover all costs? I've see Mark Chamberlain do it."

George Shadie, AEP, CLU Qualifying Member, MDRT

Let's say you have or would like to have an ideal donor, ideal client, ideal customer.

If you already have one or more ideal clients or donors, you simply duplicate that person again, and again and again, without spending any money.

If you just landed and have no one to duplicate, we can help there too.

I learned how from my grandfather.
Think Amish. Think Jabez.

I wanted individuals with the following characteristics:
1. Nice personalities
2. Money
3. Collectibles—cars, rugs, jewelry, Purdey™ shotguns, etc.
4. Charitable intent

I simply went to a friend and client who fit the profile and did what my grandfather and Jabez suggested: **I ASKED.**
1. I asked my friend and client for a hand—<u>advice, suggestions</u>.
2. I said I was planning an event and wanted to fill a room at a private club with <u>individuals like him</u>.
3. <u>Would he help</u>?
4. <u>Silence</u>. After you make the ask, be quiet. Give the person the opportunity to think about the request and how best to fill it.
5. <u>Silence</u>. After you make the ask, be quiet. Give the person the opportunity to think about the request and how best to fill it. (THIS IS NOT A TYPO. I REPEATED THIS SENTENCE BECAUSE IT IS KEY. ASK THE QUESTION AND **BE QUIET**! THEY ARE THINKING. GIVE THEM TIME.)

The results will amaze you. I sat there with my Yellow Tablet and took names. I then asked how to get in front of them and was told. We filled the ballroom at a private club with my ideal prospects. My cost was a handshake and the time it took to ask.

I now had a hot commodity—that list had value.

I cold-called Christie's™.

What If…
Christie's is 239 years old, has 53 offices in 32 countries, and I want them to send someone to Wilkes Barre and work for free?

Think Amish. Think Win-Win. Think What If.

What did I have? A room filled with wealthy individuals that had collectibles.

I told them who I was and what I wanted. (I had to repeat it a couple times—Who are you? What do you want?). I wanted a person to drive from New York City to Wilkes Barre, two hours each way, at their own expense, and speak for an hour on collectibles.

Think about what I was offering. I was going to put them in a room at a private club with wealthy people who had collectibles. The next questions I got was when and where.

I now had the prospect list and **Christie's**. What is a room filled with wealthy individuals? It is a HOT COMMODITY. It has economic value; it can be sold. Who in addition to me would like to be on the stage, in the back of the room?

I simply made a list of those businesses and started calling.

Those businesses paid for the room, the brochures, and the food.

I got new perfect prospects, the room, the food, the advertising, and Christie's with What If Thinking, a Yellow Tablet, a #2 Pencil & PhD (Pigheaded Determination®).

If you just landed, you simply approach your ideal prospect and ask. You will get turned down, you will be ignored, and you will fail—SO WHAT? You are in the game, so keep asking. Think Jabez!

What If…

12 | The Wheels on the Bus | Ideal Prospects by the Bus Load

"Get other people to fill a bus with 50 wealthy prospects, get someone to pay all costs for 18 holes on a beautiful course in the Poconos. I've seen Mark Chamberlain do it."

Joe Yenason

President, Yenason Mechanical

What If…

When I was a financial advisor, I was always interested in adding a few more ideal clients. People that make you feel good just by hearing their name. When you see their name on your phone, you smile.

Take a look at your book of business, your donor list. Is it populated with nice people, people you really enjoy?

"Fingernails on a chalkboard" is a phrase that I once used to describe my emotions when I saw some "special clients." Do you have any—or many—clients, customers, donors like that? If you do, let them go with love and replace them with your ideal clients…by the bus load.

On one of the club trips I earned at Merrill Lynch, I heard a speaker ask these questions. He asked for a volunteer to stand up and think of his favorite client, his most profitable client. He then asked that financial advisor to think of that client's occupation, hobbies, and interests. Next he asked how many clients he had who were like that. He answered that he had a few. The speaker asked why his entire book wasn't populated with people like his ideal client.

Target Marketing
We "hit" what we aim at.
Yes that's me at Paris Island in '68, "snapping in."

The first step is identifying your ideal client, customer, and donor. Where do they live? What are their interests? What do they do for a living: What do you like about them?

The next step is **Jabez: the ASK**

1. I like to play golf. I don't keep score—can't count that high.
2. I wanted to work with nice people
3. I wanted clients with $1,000,000+ in liquid investments.

What If...

I took out my Yellow Tablet & #2 Pencil and made a list of people that fit my criteria: **nice people** that **play golf** with **$1,000,000+ in liquid investments.**

I used the technique my grandfather taught me; I asked for "a hand." It went something like this: I went to the people who fit my ideal prospect profile and asked these simple questions:

1. Frank/Cindy, I need a hand with a project I'm working on. Can you help me?
2. Frank/Cindy says sure, what is it? (Remember who these people are. They know me, like me, trust me.)
3. I'm planning a _____[6] for prospective customers, people like you.
4. Who do you know, people like you, that might enjoy _____ on _____?
5. SILENCE! Let them think. The results will amaze you.

If you have no one who fits your profile, create them—**ASK**. Find out who fits your ideal profile and ask that person those questions. It is amazing what happens when we ask for help.
You will not succeed every time, but you will succeed if you continue to **ASK**.

It took several days and multiple conversations, but I got my list and introductions to the people on the list by the people who furnished their names.

The next step was the **ASK**. Not everyone said yes; many said no. I kept asking till I filled the bus.

What is a bus filled with 50 individuals who play golf with $1,000,000 liquid in investments? It is a commodity. It has value. It can be sold.

At the same time, I was lining up sponsors—individuals and companies that sold products & services my prospective clientele used.

The ASK went like this: I'm doing an event in the Poconos for 50 prospective clients; each one has an estimated $1,000,000 in investible funds. I have a limited number[7] of openings for co-sponsors. I can work you in the presentation and/or you can have a table in the back of the room. Which do you prefer? (Assume consent!)
I knew what my total cost was and then made a list, on my yellow tablet, of the people/companies that I thought would like to be in the room or on the stage with me. Again, some said no thanks or that's too much.

NEXT!

I simply continued **ASKING** until I covered the cost of the bus, the food, and the golf.

Summary: I filled a Martz bus with my ideal prospective customers. I identified and got commitments from sponsors to cover the cost of the bus, food, and golf. I got on a bus paid for by people who were eager to make that contribution—think **AMISH**. They also paid for the golf and the food. I simply showed up and continued the **ASK**.

Before we got home that evening, I got a commitment from one of my guests to become a client.

[6] Doesn't matter what you're planning. The key is the ASK.
[7] In my workshops, I teach the "**Loaf of Bread**" close. Think "limited time offer, one day only, etc.

13 | Acres of Diamonds & Glass Ceilings?

Acres of Diamonds is a book by Reverend Russell Conwell. The essence of the book is that every person, everywhere, all the time, is surrounded by opportunity.

I'll repeat that.
Every person, everywhere, all the time, is surrounded by opportunity. We just need to get off the couch and into the game every day.

Here is an example.
Lake Carey—June 2, 1998. A tornado swept through the community.
People died, homes and businesses were destroyed. Many lost everything.
Terry Martin was a single mom. She lost nearly all material possessions.

Terry Martin had an incredible advantage in her quest to bounce back and grow.

Jabez is a simple prayer about a guy with a rough beginning. He didn't quit; he asked God to bless him big time, to "expand my borders." God heard the request and granted his wish to "expand his borders."

Terry used that prayer & PhD-Pigheaded Determination® to build a national cosmetics company: Mederi Cosmetics.

After the tornado, she did an asset inventory. Her wealth was and is her family and prayer. She had both. When you lose all material wealth, Terry and I believe the only real problem you have is deciding which of the infinite opportunities that surround you to pursue.

Silos: The Idea

As a little girl, Terry liked makeup. She once traded her lunch for some makeup. Something about makeup intrigued her.

What if she could start a national cosmetics company?

She had no money, no house, few personal possessions, and young children.

Makes perfect sense to dream—e.g., **What If** she created a national cosmetics company?

Terry did not go to college. Terry got married at 17. Terry had five children. Terry wasn't afraid to ask, to fail. Think **Jabez**. She was motivated. She also had and developed a great **Vision Casting** skill coupled with **What If Thinking.**

Silos: Building | Silos: Employees | Silos: Production

In the beginning, she only knew she liked cosmetics. She invested time and effort to learn about skin, health, and cosmetics. Over time she created her own line using other people's factories to produce her product. **Think Amish**.

Silos: Marketing

She borrowed $250 to start her cosmetics company and then began selling. There are only so many hours in a day, so she did some **What If Thinking** again. What businesses deal with makeup, and could she piggyback on those businesses? She made a list of those businesses and continued selling, only now she was asking Jabez—where one yes could translate into hundreds or even thousands of orders.

Bestselling author[8] Jack Canfield suggests we consider this: when we make a sale, it can be to one person who will enjoy the book and may recommend it.

Why not make that one sale to the buyer at Macy's, Barnes & Noble, Campbell Soup, etc.? It's still one ask and one yes, but the result is DIFFERENT, HUGE, AWESOME, WOW, HOLY COW!

What If she could share her knowledge with people who could then sell her products? She approached educational institutions that deal with beauty and offered to teach, for a fee, what she had learned over years of research. Read that again. She gets paid to market her products. She doesn't pay to advertise in this channel; she gets paid to advertise, and some of those individuals then sell Terry's product line in their businesses.

Think about your product or service. Who are the consumers—HUGE CONSUMERS?

What If... Jabez

Make a list. Make the **ASK**.

Let's say you sell soap, towels, shoes, cars, books, baked goods, etc. If you ask one person and he or she says yes, you have a sale. If that person is a buyer for a store, law firm, nonprofit, or fraternal order, that sale could represent a hundred units, a thousand units, etc.

---

[8] His *Chicken Soup* series has sold over 500,000,000 copies. That's **five hundred million** books!

14 | Focus | Any Emotion, Any Time BONUS

In the '80s I took a Dale Carnegie course. One week the instructor told us to bring any newspaper to class the following week. Any newspaper.

When we arrived, he asked for a volunteer to come to the front of the room. When that person arrived, they were instructed to roll the paper up like a bat. The next instruction was to take a moment and think about that thing, person, event that upset them most and hit the table with the paper as they described in detail why they were upset. At the end of that session, "normal" people went from comfortable to rage because that's what they focused on. It was so dramatic that they no longer offer that session. They demonstrated, vividly, that any person can attain and maintain any emotion at any time. We are what we think about and focus on.

1. **Excited**: That is me leading the fans at half time at my alma mater.
2. **Grateful**: August 31, 1968. I was severely wounded near the end of a three-day battle to take a hill in Vietnam. That's me in a VA hospital. Friends were dead, missing body parts, and I would be there for months.
3. **Rage**: That's me at Paris Island. Like Dale Carnegie training, we learned how to get there in seconds.

Google **Taps the Bugler's Cry** | Listen and note how you feel.

Google **Rocky theme** | Listen and note how you feel.

Here is a bonus.
Google **Tony Robbins Alice Herz Sommer**

Put your seatbelt on. She demonstrates better than any person what I just suggested.
We are what we focus on.

15 | One in 1,000 | One in 1,000,000

1). One in 1,000!
  a. With your investment in this book, you qualify to compete for the $1,000 in 1,000 contest. I want to encourage you to employ some **What If** Thinking. Commit some time daily to think about ways to increase your:
     I. Market share
     II. Profits
     III. New products & services
  b. Submit these ideas, products, and services to me via email at markchamberlain76@gmail.com AFTER you've purchased the book.
  c. Each time I hit the 1,000th book sold & idea threshold, I will award $1,000 to the best idea, product, concept. or service.
  d. I will share all ideas with everyone who participated via an email blast and/or my webpage WhatIfU.Global.
  e. Think about what I just said. You have an opportunity to compete for $1,000 as often as you wish. Even if you lose, you win because you get to see all the ideas submitted.

2). One in 1,000,000!
  A. I need to practice what I preach. **What If**…
  B. Why not also award $1,000,000 after I hit a million book sales & ideas submitted?
  C. Invest in the book.
  D. Learn some great success strategies.
  E. Compete for $1,000,000.

3). Workshops Onsite [9]: Your Business, Nonprofit, or Community Event
  a. One hour: $1,500–$2,500*
     I. The Brain: **What If** Thinking, **Vision Casting**
     II. The Amish: Relationship-Based Business Building
     III. Food, Sex, Money: Turn People on with a Series of Three-Word Phrases
     IV. *Invest an additional $1,000 and get an extra hour of Brainstorming with $1,000 for best idea
  b. Four Hours: $5,000–$6,000*
     I. The Brain: **What If** Thinking, **Vision Casting**
     II. The Amish: Relationship-Based Business Building
     III. Food, Sex, Money: Turn People on with a Series of Three-Word Phrases
     IV. Client Copier, Donor Duplication
     V. Secret Silos
     VI. Cosmic Board
     VII. An Example
     VIII. "Live" Session Where We Walk through an Audience-Suggested Challenge
     IX. *Invest an additional $1,000 and get an extra hour of Brainstorming with $1,000 for best idea

4). Custom Workshops
  Don't see what you need? Let's talk. 570-262-6261

---

[9] These prices include travel within Pennsylvania, New York & New Jersey.
Call 570-262-6261 or email markchamberlain76@gmail.com for a quote outside that area.

Special Thanks

This project has been a team effort, and I'd like to acknowledge that effort. The four key players are successful in their own right.

I'd like you to "meet" them. I recommend each and all wholeheartedly:

Terry Martin

Founder, Mederi Cosmetics

http://www.medericosmetics

Donna LaBar

Nutritional Healing Coach

http://www.donnalabar.com

Jeramie-Scott Cannella

Mederi Skin Care President

http://www.mederiskincare.com/

Jassen Popp

Creator, American QR Code

http://www.popabroad.com/

www.ingramcontent.com/pod-product-compliance
Lightning Source LLC
Chambersburg PA
CBHW042029150426
43198CB00003B/105